WRITE

99 Photos to Inspire Writing

what you

SEE

Hank Kellner

Cottonwood Press, Inc.

W9-BON-124

Cottonwood Press, Inc.
109-B Cameron Drive
Fort Collins, Colorado 80525
www.cottonwoodpress.com
1-800-864-4297

ISBN 978-1-877673-83-2

Library of Congress Control Number: 2008938630

Printed in the United States of America

Cover design by Anne Marie Martinez

All photography is by author Hank Kellner, unless otherwise indicated.

The author's blog:
www.hank-englisheducation.blogspot.com

TABLE OF CONTENTS

ACKNOWLEDGMENTS

The author would like to thank the individuals listed below.

- **Elizabeth Guy**, for encouragement and inspiration

- **Kerri Blankenship**, for help with student photography

- **Cheryl Thurston and her staff**, for careful revision and editing

- The following, for use of additional photos: **Tom Beckett; Mary Calderia; Denver Public Library, Western History Collection; Elizabeth Guy; George Junne; Melissa Lawson; Alice Lin; Paige Mosier; Mark Parkhurst; Sunita Pathik; Julia Stein; Wendy Valdez; and Sarah Waterworth**

- The following educators for their suggestions and support:

    Mary Birky, Papillion-La Vista High School, Papillion, Nebraska

    Carol Booth Olson, Director, UCI Writing Project (University of California—Irvine); National Writing Project Advisory Board

    Martin Brandt, Independence High School, San Jose, California

    Ann Cox, Consultant, Illinois State Writing Project

    James Davis, Director, Iowa Writing Project

    Linda Dick, Kalamazoo Valley Community College, Kalamazoo, Michigan

    Joann Garbarini, Irvine High School, Irvine, California

    Peter Golden, South Boston High School, Boston, Massachusetts

    Frank Holes, Jr., Editor, *Star Teaching*, Indian River, Michigan

    Amber Luck, Hennepin Technical College, Brooklyn Park, Minnesota

    Mary Lee Meyer, Consultant, Prairie Lands Writing Project, Missouri Western State University, St. Joseph, Missouri

    Kathy Miller, West Platte High School, Weston, Missouri

    Allison Movitz, Special Programs Coordinator, University of Mississippi Writing Project

Barbara Raney, California State University—Monterey Bay, California

Valerie Reimers, Southwestern Oklahoma State University, Weatherford, Oklahoma

Alisa Santti, Ottawa Elementary School, Petoskey, Michigan

Derri Scarlett, Bismarck State College, Bismarck, North Dakota

Diane Sekeres, Director, Longleaf Writing Project, University of Alabama

Jennifer Sluss, Co-Director, Mountain Writing Project, Hazard Community and Technical College, Hazard, Kentucky

Justin Van Kleeck, Former Adjunct Assistant Professor of English, Piedmont Virginia Community College

Kristy Weidner-Gonzalez, Co-Director, Lehigh Valley Writing Project, Pennsylvania State University

Patricia West, Department Head, Savannah Technical College; Affiliate, Georgia SouthernWriting Project

TEN WAYS TO USE *WRITE WHAT YOU SEE*

Imagination is a powerful force. But sometimes imagination needs a little help to get it going. That's when photography can be useful in the classroom. *Write What You See* is a collection of black and white photographs that is designed to stimulate writing while offering maximum flexibility to both you and your students.

Each page of the text presents one or more photographs accompanied by at least one quotation that will help to kindle your students' imaginations while providing them with many ideas for writing.

The pages vary, with every page including some, but not all, of the following: possible key words, questions to consider, ideas for writing, possible opening lines, suggestions for researching and writing, and other prompts to help provide more guidance and inspiration.

The CD that accompanies the book includes all the activities in *Write What You See*. It allows you to project activities from the book, or you can choose to show only photos, without the text.

Many of the entries in *Write What You See* offer opportunities for students to write narrative pieces. Others lend themselves to expository pieces. Some require research. If you wish, you can emphasize the use of analysis, comparison and contrast, chronological order, cause and effect, spatial relationships, and/or process analysis as techniques for organizing writing.

But you may also, if you wish, encourage students to ignore the written prompts, study the photos, and use their imaginations as guides. By doing so, they will discover a rich source of ideas that will certainly help to overcome any reluctance they may have about writing.

The possibilities for using *Write What You See* to stimulate writing are endless and limited only by a teacher's imagination and creativity. Below are ten possible approaches.

1. **Specific skills.** Decide on a specific skill you wish to teach, such as writing dialogue or description. After a lesson and class discussion on the skill, have students write about a photo, applying the skill.

2. **Creative group work.** Divide the class into groups and distribute photocopies of selected pages from *Write What You See*. Allow time for students to exchange ideas about the photos without your direction. Then have each group choose a photo and come up with a written creative response. Several students might wish to work together to write a one-act play, for example. Others might collaborate on a song, an editorial, or a commercial. Encourage students to use their imaginations in a collaborative effort, but allow students who prefer to work alone to do so.

3. **Role playing.** Have volunteers act out one or more of the situations presented in different photographs. Then assign compositions based on the students' responses to both the dramatizations and the photographs.

4. **Newspaper reports.** Assign different photos to individual students and ask them to write news articles based on what might be happening in the photos. Use the articles to publish a class newspaper based on the photos.

5. **Different points of view.** Assign pairs of students to work together on a single photograph that shows two or more faces or figures. Allow them to discuss their interpretations of the photograph. Then have each student choose one of the people in the photograph and write about what is happening, assuming that person's point of view.

6. **Illustrated anthology.** Ask students to photograph people, places, or things they observe in the world around them. Use the photographs as stimuli for discussion, and then ask students to write compositions based on their responses to the photos. Finally, have them create an illustrated anthology using both text and photos.

7. **Poetry anthologies.** Ask students to select several photographs that appeal to the five senses. Then have them discuss the photographs. What can they see? If they were "inside" the photo, what would they hear, feel, taste, smell? Have students compile a list of responses. Then ask them to write poems or brief descriptive pieces using as many of the five senses as possible.

8. **Descriptive writing.** Choose two photos, each showing one individual. Ask students to describe both individuals as completely as possible. Who could they be? What are they like? What are they doing? Another approach is to ask students to compare and contrast the individuals in each photo.

9. **Creative responses.** After students have written pieces based on any of the photographs in this collection, have them exchange papers and read each other's work. Ask students to write a brief response to each paper read—either a positive comment, a question, or a suggestion.

10. **Fiction.** Have students write a short story based on a photo in *Write What You See*. Or, if time is short, have them create just one element of the story. They might describe the setting in detail, as well as why they have chosen such a setting. They might write a character study of the protagonist or the antagonist. They might describe the main conflict of the story. They might describe the resolution. Or they might write a synopsis of the story.

For even more ideas, see "How Some Teachers Use Photographs to Inspire Writing," page 113.

PHOTOS and WRITING PROMPTS

"The debt we owe to the play of imagination is incalculable."

Carl Jung
Swiss psychiatrist

QUESTIONS TO CONSIDER

- Does the photo show a sunrise or a sunset?

- Is the person male or female?

- Is the tone of the photo positive or negative, in your opinion? Do you sense hope, fear, determination, or...?

POSSIBLE OPENING LINES

- It was like a bad dream come true...

- Who was he? What did he want?...

- The mysterious intruder appeared out of nowhere...

"I wasted time, and now doth time waste me."

William Shakespeare
British playwright

IDEAS FOR WRITING

- What is time, really? Suppose you had to explain it to someone who didn't understand. What would you say?

- When does time seem to stand still for you? When does it fly?

- If you could relive a moment in time, what moment would it be? What would you change? What would you keep the same?

- What does it mean to "waste" time? What does it mean to "manage" it?

- Imagine that you can travel into the past or future and then come back to the present. Where will you go? Why?

"Man's life is like a drop of dew on a leaf."

Socrates
Greek philosopher

IDEAS FOR WRITING

• As you look at the photo, jot down all the words and phrases that come to mind. Write as quickly as possible, without judging what you are writing. After you have a long list, choose from these words and phrases to create a poem.

• Compare and/or contrast the leaf shown in the photo with something else in nature.

• The photo shows a close-up of a leaf. With words, create a close-up of something else from nature. Use as many of the five senses as you can.

• In the quotation above, what do you think Socrates means?

"They say a reasonable number of fleas is good for a dog—keeps him from broodin' over bein' a dog."

Edward Noyes Westcott
American author

QUESTIONS TO CONSIDER

- Why are people so attracted to dogs? What is their appeal?

- Why do perfect strangers feel comfortable approaching a stranger with a dog?

- What do puppies and babies have in common?

POSSIBLE OPENING LINES

- A dog I'll never forget was...

- I think I'm jealous of my dog...

- Foo-Foo was a little princess...

- If I ever own a dog in the future, it will be a...

"Appearances often are deceiving."
Aesop
Greek slave-storyteller

IDEAS FOR WRITING

Is the bottle in this photo a giant bottle placed on a street to advertise a product? Or is it a replica placed in a miniature setting with other models?

Actually, it is neither. Though it does advertise Coke, it is really a semi-glass building in Las Vegas that formerly housed the World of Coca-Cola museum, now closed.

- When have you found appearances to be deceiving? Describe an incident.

- Write a fable with the moral, "Appearances are often deceiving."

- Write a story in which you find yourself surrounded by objects and buildings that are much larger than they normally are.

"Never fight an inanimate object."

P. J. O'Rourke
American journalist and author

IDEAS FOR WRITING

- Imagine that you are one of the figures in the photos, above, or that you are some other nonhuman figure. Describe your new "self" fully. Tell about your size, your shape, your abilities. Can you move? Can you communicate with humans? Do you have special powers? Did you arrive on Earth from another planet, or were you created here?

- Imagine that you discover you have the power to become an object that is not human for twenty-four hours only. Write about your experience.

"The face is the mirror of the mind, and eyes without speaking confess the secrets of the heart."

Saint Jerome
Roman Catholic saint

IDEAS FOR WRITING

- What do you think you know about this woman, just from looking at her face? Explain.

- Do you agree that eyes can "confess the secrets of the heart?" Explain.

- Imagine the secrets that might lie behind this woman's eyes.

- Imagine that this woman is a character in a story you are writing. Create a character sketch describing her.

POSSIBLE KEY WORDS

SINCERITY   LOVE   TRUTH   SECRETS

*"Pain is temporary.
Quitting lasts forever."*

Lance Armstrong
American athlete

RESEARCH AND WRITE

The athlete above has undoubtedly encountered pain in his training, as all athletes do. Some athletes, however, have had more than their share. For example, Tenley Albright had polio as a child, but she went on to become the first American woman to win an Olympic Gold Medal in figure skating at the 1956 Olympics. After suffering a severely sprained ankle and a fractured fibula on December 19, 2004, Philadelphia Eagles football player Terrell Owens went on to play in Super Bowl XXXIX. Cyclist Lance Armstrong underwent treatment for cancer at one point in his career but recovered and went on to win the grueling Tour de France seven consecutive times from 1999-2005.

Discuss the lives of several athletes who have succeeded in spite of severe illness or injuries. What happened to them? How did they overcome their problems?

POSSIBLE OPENING LINES

- I am not a quitter...

- The first time I competed in...

"Each tree grows alone,
murmurs alone,
thinks alone."

Willa Cather
American author

POSSIBLE OPENING LINES

- Lost in the woods, the traveler looked up to see...

- A solitary tree stood at the edge of a meadow...

- I am a tree...

- A cold wind attacked the tree and the men who shivered beneath its branches...

- When she saw the bare branches of the tree outlined against the sky, the girl wished that...

- They decided to meet under the tree...

POSSIBLE KEY WORDS

BARE   BEAUTIFUL   STARK   LONELY   INTRICATE

"Every man's work, whether it be literature or music or pictures or architecture or anything else, is always a portrait of himself."

Samuel Butler
British poet and satirist

QUESTIONS TO CONSIDER

- What could the man be looking at so intently?

- What is in the background? Where do you think the photo was taken?

- What would you guess the man does for a living, based on the photo?

POSSIBLE OPENING LINES

- The look in the man's eyes told David he had gone too far...

- Before he became a stock broker, Tate had a secret past...

"You cannot open a book without learning something."

Confucius
Chinese philosopher

IDEAS FOR WRITING

• The girl in the photo appears to be lost in a book. When have you been lost in a book? What was the book? What was it about the book that captured your attention?

• How do books tap the imagination?

• Describe a favorite fictional character, emotionally as well as physically. Tell how your character deals with important conflicts or problems in the book.

POSSIBLE OPENING LINES

• She heard nothing, saw nothing—except for the page before her...

• "That character is exactly like me," Kate thought...

"Here is the place! American history shall march along that skyline."

Gutzon Borglum
Sculptor, Mount Rushmore

RESEARCH AND WRITE

There are 44 National Memorials in the United States, but perhaps the most impressive one is Mount Rushmore. It features the faces of Presidents George Washington, Thomas Jefferson, Abraham Lincoln, and Theodore Roosevelt. The creator, Gutzon Borglum, chose these presidents because of their importance in the first 150 years of American history.

- Describe the creation of the Mount Rushmore National Memorial. What problems were encountered in its creation? How were they overcome?

- Find out about the creation of the Crazy Horse memorial, near Mount Rushmore.

- Select any other national memorial, describe it, and discuss its significance to our nation.

POSSIBLE OPENING LINE

- If I could add another former president to the Mount Rushmore National Memorial, I would choose...

"Share our similarities, celebrate our differences."

M. Scott Peck
American psychiatrist

IDEAS FOR WRITING

* Is the protester male or female? Does it matter that the protester has hidden his or her identity?

* What do you think about the quotation on the sign? Is it true or false?

* If you could talk to the person in the photograph, what would you say?

* Is there a cause you care a lot about? How far would you go to stand up for what you believe?

* In your opinion, are demonstrations effective? Why or why not?

RESEARCH AND WRITE

* Find out about significant demonstrations that have taken place in our country. Choose one and describe it.

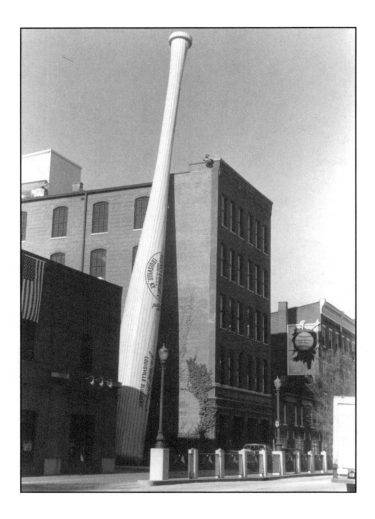

"But there is no joy in Mudville—
mighty Casey has struck out."

from "Casey at the Bat"
Ernest Lawrence Thayer
American poet

IDEAS FOR WRITING

• Whose baseball bat is it? Write a tall tale that features a giant baseball bat.

• What is the most exciting baseball game you have ever participated in or watched? Describe it.

• Who is your favorite baseball player? Why?

• Baseball has long been called "America's pastime." Now many say football has replaced it as America's favorite sport. What do you think?

"Boys wear their hearts on their sleeves. Even when they're trying to pull one over on you, they're so transparent."

Patricia Heaton
American actor

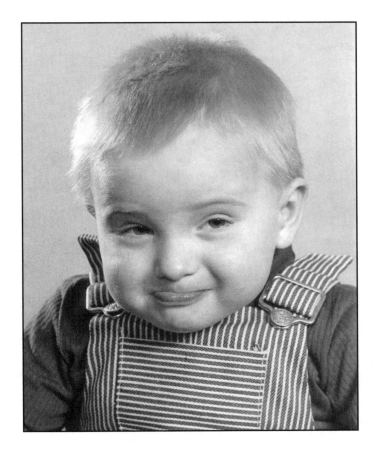

QUESTIONS TO CONSIDER

- What does the look on the boy's face mean? What might have led up to such an expression?

- Can you come up with some suitable captions for the photo?

POSSIBLE OPENING LINES

- What makes you think I stole the cookies?...

- Ms. Anderson had three "easy" children. And then there was Andrew...

- "I didn't do it!" Jeremy insisted as his mother pointed to the...

"Life is like an onion: You peel it off one layer at a time, and sometimes you weep."

Carl Sandburg
American poet

IDEAS FOR WRITING

- Describe an onion to someone who has never seen or tasted one.

- Reveal what an onion would say if it could express its feelings.

- Imagine that you are an onion that is about to be sliced onto a hamburger.

POSSIBLE OPENING LINES

- "Oh, no," I shouted as a hand holding a sharp knife began to descend on me...

- People certainly seem to have strong opinions about me...

- It all depends on your point of view. An onion is like...

*"A happy family is but
an earlier heaven."*

George Bernard Shaw
Irish playwright

IDEAS FOR WRITING

- What can you tell about the family, based on the picture alone? What can you tell about the various family members?

- What if the people in this photo could tell you what they were thinking when the picture was taken? What do you think they might say?

- Create a conversation that you imagine could have taken place between two members of this family.

- Write a paragraph that reveals what might have taken place before or after this photo was taken.

POSSIBLE KEY WORDS

FAMILY   MEMORIES   ANCESTORS   SIBLINGS   PARENTS

"A mother always has to think twice, once for herself and once for her child."

Sophia Loren
Italian actor

IDEAS FOR WRITING

- Imagine what the mother in this photo might be thinking. Or is she a sister? In a short paper, describe her thoughts.

- Recall a memorable moment from childhood that you shared with your mother. Describe the moment.

- Can mothers ever be too caring? Too attentive? Too loving? Explain.

POSSIBLE KEY WORDS

LOVE   CARING   GUIDANCE   COMPASSION

"The gift of fantasy has meant more
to me than my talent for absorbing
positive knowledge."

Albert Einstein
German physicist

IDEAS FOR WRITING

- What if the statues shown in this photo suddenly came to life? Describe the scene.

- What if the woman believes that she can communicate with the statues? Describe what might happen.

- What if the statues can see and hear what is going on around them? Write a scene where the statues interact with their surroundings.

POSSIBLE KEY WORDS

PRETENDING   CHANGING   FANTASIZING   CONTRASTING

> *"To know is nothing at all;*
> *to imagine is everything."*
>
> Anatole France
> French author

IDEAS FOR WRITING

- Two railroad trains on a collision course...

- A journey to an exotic location...

- Standing alone in a railroad station...

- A train that is always late...

- Waiting for a train that never arrives...

- A chance meeting on a train...

- Somewhere, a stalled car on the tracks...

"We got into all the trouble you could ever imagine."

Quincy Jones
American musician

IDEAS FOR WRITING

- Describe what is happening in the photo, using all five senses. What do the boys see, hear, smell, feel, taste? Make your description as vivid as possible.

- Tell about an experience you or a friend had at a river, lake, swimming pool, or beach.

- Create a story in which a water sport that involves having fun suddenly becomes dangerous.

- What activity represents "summer" to you?

POSSIBLE OPENING LINES

- I remember the time when I was swimming and...

- Sadly, the children didn't know about the undertow...Or the sharks...Or the...

"You might be a king or a little street sweeper, but sooner or later, you dance with the reaper."

Grim Reaper
Character in *Bill & Ted's Bogus Journey*

IDEAS FOR WRITING

Did you know that death is one of the most frequently discussed subjects in literature? Whether it appears as a symbol, a theme, a plot, or even a character, death has fascinated writers for many thousands of years.

• Imagine that you are walking through the cemetery. What thoughts might be going through your mind?

• Imagine that you are alone in the cemetery after dark. What thoughts might be going through your mind?

POSSIBLE OPENING LINES

• I looked at the dates on the headstones, and my heart froze...

• Yes, it was a ghost...

• Harry and Sophie hadn't intended to stay at the graveyard after dark, but...

"I let him take me for a ride
On a giant Ferris wheel
Up in the neon sky..."

Joni Mitchell
Canadian musician

IDEAS FOR WRITING

- Pictured above, the Wonder Wheel at Coney Island, New York, stands 150 feet high. How does it feel to sit high above the crowd in a Ferris wheel? Include details about sensory impressions—sounds, sights, tastes, etc.

- What if the Ferris wheel in the photo broke down and stopped? Describe what it might be like to be the person stranded in the air.

- Describe your favorite part of your favorite amusement park. What do you like about it?

RESEARCH AND WRITE

- Find out about the London Eye, the Star of Nanchang, Voyager Observation Wheel, and other Ferris wheels worldwide. Describe them.

- Find out about the invention of the Ferris wheel. Who created it? When? Why?

"Courage is being afraid but going on anyhow."

Dan Rather
American journalist

IDEAS FOR WRITING

Look at the details. What do you think is happening in the photo? Now imagine that a problem is suddenly *added* to the scene above. Write about one of the "What if?" questions below, or think of a "What if?" question of your own:

- What if the helicopter suddenly loses power?
- What if one of the onlookers falls overboard?
- What if the line attached to the rescuer breaks?
- What if a storm arrives?
- What if the call for help turns out to be a false alarm?
- What if someone in the scene suddenly loses courage?
- What if you are the person hanging from the helicopter? What do you see, feel, hear? What thoughts are going through your mind?

POSSIBLE KEY WORDS

COURAGE   DANGER   RISK   EXCITEMENT

"Every doorway, every intersection has a story."

Katherine Dunn
American author

IDEAS FOR WRITING

- Describe the young man. Why is he standing in the doorway? What could he be thinking? As he looks off to the side, what does he see?

- Imagine what might have happened before the young man came to stand in this doorway, or imagine what might happen in the next few moments. Describe the scene you imagine.

POSSIBLE OPENING LINES

- Framed in a darkened doorway, the young man looks off to the side and sees...

- He didn't know how long he had been standing there. He had lost track of time...

POSSIBLE KEY WORDS

WAITING   HOPING   THINKING   REMEMBERING   SEEING

*"And I'm proud to be an American, where at least I know I'm free.
And I won't forget the men who died who gave that right to me."*

Lee Greenwood
American singer-songwriter

IDEAS FOR WRITING

- Look at the photo. What might the man be thinking as he looks at all the names? What would *you* be thinking?

- Find out about any member of the United States Armed Forces who served at any time in our country's history. Write a story, poem, or brief biography in which you memorialize the person's service to the United States.

- What does it mean to "serve" your country?

RESEARCH AND WRITE

- Find out about the history of Memorial Day. When did it originate? Why is it sometimes known as "Decoration Day"?

"There is only one pretty child in the world, and every mother has it."
Chinese proverb

IDEAS FOR WRITING

- If babies have thoughts, what might be going through the mind of the baby in the photo? Do you think babies do have thoughts?

- Sometimes our best "mothering" comes from someone other than our actual mother. Has someone other than (or in addition to) your mother filled a mothering role in your life?

- Discuss several characteristics of your mother that you admire.

- Is there anything you wish your mother would not do?

- What do you think is the most important thing for a mother to remember? How about a father? Why?

- What do you think is the most important thing for a mother never to do? And a father? Why?

"A lonely man is a lonesome thing..."
John Cheever
American author

IDEAS FOR WRITING

• What does the man's body language tell you? What are the possibilities?

• If you sat next to the man in the photo and he was awake, what questions would you ask him?

• How does it feel to be alone?

POSSIBLE OPENING LINES

• Alfonse couldn't take another step...

• Nobody knew what had happened, and he swore no one would ever know...

POSSIBLE KEY WORDS

WEARY   THOUGHTFUL   ALONE   ISOLATED   GRIEVING

"Everyone has ancestors and it is only a question of going back far enough to find a good one."

Howard Kenneth Nixon
British author

IDEAS FOR WRITING

- Imagine the story behind the photo. Who could the people be, and what is their relationship? What kind of person is each? What are they doing together? Who is taking the photo?

- What do you know about your own ancestors? Is there someone famous in your family tree? A black sheep? A war hero? A talented woman? A pioneer? Or...? Tell about one of your ancestors.

- Many families have a characteristic that identifies them, generation after generation. The Millers might identify themselves as honest, hard-working folks. The Montanados might think of themselves as people who value education highly. The Johnsons might think of themselves as fun-loving and happy-go-lucky. What trait is characteristic of your family?

"I read the newspapers avidly. It is my one form of continuous fiction."

Aneurin Bevan
British politician

IDEAS FOR WRITING

• Why are the men in the photos reading outside? What do you think they are reading?

• Based on the photos alone, how would you guess the two men are different? Alike?

• Create a newspaper story about one of the men. Remember that newspaper style involves telling the basics right away: Who? What? When? Where? How?

POSSIBLE OPENING LINES

• The two men were alike, and yet they were different...

• Henry read everything he could get his hands on. Everything...

"Life is partly what we make it, and partly what is made by the friends we choose."

Tennessee Williams
American playwright

IDEAS FOR WRITING

- Imagine that the men in the photo are characters in a movie. What roles are they playing? How do they interact with one another?

- Discuss the quotation below the photo. Do you agree? Disagree? Why or why not?

- Describe one of your friends. What characteristics do you like about him or her?

- Tell about a time when a friend let you down.

- Tell about a time when a friend helped you overcome a difficult situation.

- To what extent do friends influence each other? Give specific examples.

*"Those twin towers
Standing tall with pride,
Fell with grieving hearts.
Stunned, America cried.
But we're still standing."*

Hannah Schoechert
7th grade student, 2001

IDEA FOR WRITING

- Since the terrorist attack of September 11, 2001, images of the twin towers at the World Trade Center generally bring up strong feelings. What emotion is strongest for you?

RESEARCH AND WRITE

- Find out about and describe any act of heroism that firefighters or police officers performed on 9/11/2001.

- In addition to the tragic loss of life in the 9/11 attack, many valuable records, archives, paintings, sculptures, and photographs were lost. Also lost were artifacts from an 18th century African burial ground. Find out more about the African Burial Ground National Monument. Why is the site historically significant?

"The real magic wand is the child's own mind."

José Ortega y Gasset
Spanish philosopher

IDEAS FOR WRITING

- Recall an incident from your childhood that was magical.

- Describe a game you played when you were a child. Did you play alone? With others? What did you like about the game?

- Did you have imaginary friends as a child? Tell about what you remember.

- Did you have any unusual habits as a child?

POSSIBLE OPENING LINES

- When I was a small child, I liked to pretend that I was a...

- I remember the time in school when I...

- When I was little, my imagination sometimes got me into trouble...

"When I grow up I want to be a little boy."

Joseph Heller
American author

IDEAS FOR WRITING

• The little boy in this picture is probably waiting for his mother to finish washing clothes at the Laundromat. But what does he see? What could he be watching? What could he be thinking about? Write the thoughts that you imagine might be in the little boy's head.

• What if...

...an accident occurred outside the window?

...he saw an ice cream truck approaching?

...the boy's mother left the Laundromat without him?

...he saw a crime taking place and no one believed him?

...he was fascinated with a worker jackhammering the street and wandered out to watch?

"All the guys who can paint great big pictures can paint great small ones."

Ernest Hemingway
American author

IDEAS FOR WRITING

- If you were present at this scene, what would you say to the two artists?

- Create a conversation that might take place—between the two artists or between the man at the left and the two artists.

- What is your opinion of the artwork itself? State reasons for your response.

- What is your definition of art? Explain.

"I look out the window sometimes to seek the color of the shadows..."

Grandma Moses
American artist

IDEAS FOR WRITING

- In the photo, a plant is silhouetted in the window, and light creates a pattern on the curtain. Imagine what lies on one side of the window, inside the room. Or imagine what lies on the other side of the window, outside the room.

- Look at the photo with "new eyes" and imagine that what you see is not a plant in a window but something else. Describe what it could be.

- Describe a scene as you see it from any window in your home or another structure.

- Imagine someone looking into a window and discovering something strange, dangerous, surprising, or important. What happens?

"Archaeology is the peeping Tom of the sciences."

Jim Bishop
American journalist

IDEA FOR WRITING

*   Famed archeologist Louisiana Bones and his companion, Darlene Daring, discover three tablets in the Sahara Desert. After deciphering the code, pictured above, they set out to find the long lost Temple of Gloom. Write the story of "Louisiana Bones and the Temple of Gloom," telling about their epic journey to the Temple.

QUESTIONS TO CONSIDER

As you write "Louisiana Bones and the Temple of Gloom," be sure to consider the following:

*   What is the meaning of the code?

*   Who are your main characters, and what are they like? Create a vivid picture of them.

*   Where does your story take place? Be sure to describe the setting.

*   What is the main conflict in the story? Make sure this conflict is resolved by the end of the story.

*   Who are the villains in your story?

"Just living is not enough. One must have sunshine, freedom, and a little flower."

Hans Christian Andersen
Danish author

IDEAS FOR WRITING

- What words come to mind as you look at the photo? Describe the flowers in terms of sight, touch, and smell.

- Why do flowers give people pleasure? Discuss several ways.

- Compare and contrast two well-known paintings that feature flowers.

- So many poets have used flowers as a subject for their work. Try your hand at a poem about a flower.

- If you were a flower, what kind would you be? Why?

POSSIBLE KEY WORDS

DELICATE   FRAGRANT   FRAGILE   SCENTED   VIBRANT

"I got vision and the rest of the world wears bifocals."

Butch Cassidy
in the movie
Butch Cassidy and the Sundance Kid

IDEAS FOR WRITING

When you look through binoculars, the world is at your fingertips. Objects in the distance appear to be much larger than they actually are. You can see for miles.

- What if, when you looked through binoculars, you could see only the good things in life? Or only the bad things in life?

- Imagine what it would be like to be able to see things clearly at great distances without using binoculars. What are some ways in which you would use your extraordinary vision? What would be the benefits? Would there be any disadvantages?

POSSIBLE OPENING LINES

- If I live to be a hundred, I never want to see...

- Let me describe the scene...

"Sometimes dreams alter the course of an entire life."

Judith Duerk
American psychotherapist-author

IDEAS FOR WRITING

- Is the woman in the photo dreaming? Thinking? Staring? What do you think her eyes reveal?

- Write a story or poem in which a dream plays an important part. Describe the dream vividly.

POSSIBLE OPENING LINES

- The look on her face haunted him, haunted them all...

- Her eyes were on the scene in front of her, but her mind was a million miles away...

- Angela woke up in a strange place...

"Life is a mystery as deep as ever death can be..."

Mary Mapes Dodge
American author

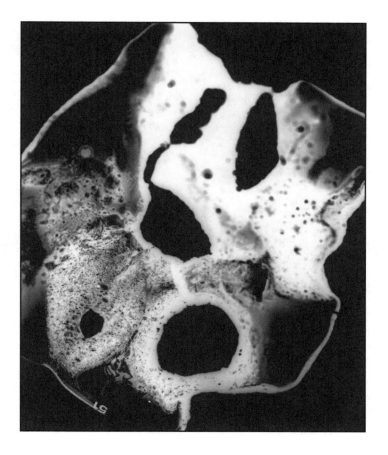

IDEAS FOR WRITING

- Study the photo. What do you think it is? Give reasons for your choice.

- For three minutes, write down everything that comes to mind as you look at the photo. What words come to mind? What emotions? Questions? Fantasies? Look over what you have written. Choose something from your work and use it as the basis for a paragraph.

- Imagine that you are walking along a trail in the woods when you see a strange object off to the side. Curious to find out what the object is, you stop, bend over to pick it up, and then recoil when you see that the object is a...

POSSIBLE OPENING LINES

- The planet was nothing like Earth...

- They all stared at the object that landed at their feet...

"Gentlemen of the jury... The one absolute, unselfish friend that man can have in this selfish world—the one that never deserts him, the one that never proves ungrateful or treacherous—is his dog."

George Graham Vest
American lawyer-politician

IDEAS FOR WRITING

- Is the dog in the photo resting? Waiting? Or...? How would you describe the dog?

- Describe a dog that proved to be exceptionally loyal to you. How did it show its loyalty?

- Describe a dog you have loved.

RESEARCH AND WRITE

There are hundreds of true-life stories about dogs that remained faithful to their owners. One was Hachiko, an Akita dog whose master died on May 21, 1925, at a ceremony he was attending at a Tokyo railway station. According to observers, the next day and for nine more years Hachiko returned to the station and waited for his master before walking home alone.

Search the Internet for more information about two or more service dogs, military dogs, police dogs, or rescue dogs. Describe your choices and tell about how they demonstrated loyalty and devotion to their owners. Be sure to use specific examples.

"Memory is a child walking along a seashore. You never can tell what small pebble it may pick up and store away among its treasured things."
Pierce Harris
American clergyman

IDEAS FOR WRITING

• What if one of the boys finds a message in a bottle?

• What if an offshore swimmer cries out for help?

• What if lightning begins to strike the water near the boys?

• What if the boys discover something fascinating or frightening that has washed ashore?

POSSIBLE OPENING LINES

• Moving quickly, Morgan bent to pick up a small, shiny object in the sand...

• Jake thought his brother was right behind him, but when he turned...

• The boys soon realized they had walked too far along the beach...

• The boys were enjoying their Saturday when...

"Boys are perhaps beyond the range of anybody's sure understanding, at least when they are between the ages of eighteen months and ninety years."

James Thurber
American humorist and cartoonist

POSSIBLE OPENING LINES

- "Do you see what I see?" he asked...

- The boys stood and waited as the stranger approached them.

- "We've got time," he said, relaxing...

- "What do you want to do today?" James asked his older brother.

"…don't let us rejoice in punishment…"

George Eliot
British author

IDEAS FOR WRITING

- Stocks, shown above, were used in Puritan times as a form of punishment and humiliation. Do you think humiliation should be a part of punishment?

- How do you think teachers and school administrators should discipline or punish unruly students?

- Do you believe that capital punishment is an effective way of dealing with convicted murderers? Defend or attack that form of punishment. Give reasons for your position.

"I suppose I've passed it a hundred times, but I always stop for a minute And look at the house, the tragic house, the house with nobody in it."

Joyce Kilmer
from "The House with Nobody in It"
American journalist and poet

IDEAS FOR WRITING

- Imagine what the building in the photo might have been at one time. What might have led to its current state?

- What if you wanted to seek shelter from the rain in the building but your intuition told you not to enter it?

- What if someone appeared at one the windows and cried out for help?

POSSIBLE OPENING LINES

- At first I thought that the building was deserted, but when I got closer to it...

- She had never thought of a building as having feelings, but...

"Other things may change us, but we start and end with family."

Anthony Brandt
American music educator

QUESTIONS TO CONSIDER

• Observe the people in the photo carefully. Who do you think they might be? What can you guess about them, based on the photograph alone?

• Imagine where the photo was taken. What sounds might be in the background? What smells? What objects might be found near the individuals?

IDEA FOR WRITING

After you have answered the questions above, use the information you have provided to create a "scene" involving the people in the photo. What happened before the photo? What happened afterwards?

If you like, expand your scene into an entire short story. (If you do, remember that every story needs conflict. What difficulties will your characters face?)

"A knight there was, and that a worthy man,
That from the time he first began
To riden out, he loved chivalry,
Truth and honour, freedom and courtesy . . .
At mortal battles had he fought fifteen . . .
And each time slain his foe . . .
He was a truly perfect, gentle knight."

Geoffrey Chaucer
from the Prologue to *The Canterbury Tales*
British author

IDEAS FOR WRITING

- Describe the action in the photo as if you were reporting on a modern sporting event. Be sure to use active verbs.

- Look at Chaucer's words, above, from the Middle Ages. How do you imagine someone could be a "truly perfect, gentle knight" while slaying "his foe"?

- If a medieval knight were to watch television today, what do you imagine he would think of what he sees?

- People often say that chivalry is "dead." Is it?

> *"Sentences that begin with 'all women' are never, never true."*
> Margaret Culkin Banning
> American author

IDEAS FOR WRITING

- Study the women in the photo. Though they are from different countries, what do you imagine they might have in common?

- If they could speak the same language, what might the women shown in these photos discuss over lunch?

- Do you think people make assumptions about others, based on their gender?

"Immigration is the sincerest form of flattery."

Jack Paar
American entertainer

IDEAS FOR WRITING

- Who is the man in the photo standing against a background of rugs, a for sale sign, an American flag, and several other objects? Is he a U.S. citizen whose family has been in the country for generations? Is he a visitor to the U.S.? Is he a recent immigrant?

  He could, of course, be any of the above. Write a dramatic monologue in which the man tells the story of his life, as you imagine it.

- Discuss some of the problems a newcomer to this country would be likely to have.

- Describe in detail the setting in which the man finds himself.

- To what degree should the U.S. accommodate non-English speakers? Should signs be in more than one language? Should ballots be available in several languages? Should English classes for non-native speakers be taught in public schools?

- Do you think everyone should learn a second language?

> *"Music was my refuge. I could crawl into the space between the notes and curl my back to loneliness."*
>
> Maya Angelou
> American poet

IDEAS FOR WRITING

- What kind of music do you imagine the person in the photo is playing? Describe it.

- Is music ever *your* refuge?

- If you could set some thoughts to music, what thoughts would you choose?

- What is one of your favorite songs? What appeals to you about it? What effect does the song have on you? Be specific.

"Home is home, be it ever so humble."
Old proverb

SOME FACTS TO CONSIDER

- 3.5 million people will experience homelessness in a given year.
- 1.35 million of these people will be children.
- 43% of the homeless population consists of women.
- Families with children comprise 33% of the homeless population.
- Veterans constitute 40% of the homeless population.
- 1 in every 5 homeless persons has a severe or persistent mental illness.

Source: Los Angeles Homeless Coalition Services, 2007

RESEARCH AND WRITE

- How are various cities around the country approaching the problem of homelessness?
- How is the problem of homelessness handled where you live?
- What are some of the causes of homelessness?
- How does homelessness affect other people in a community?
- What organizations help the homeless? Choose one and find out what it does, specifically.

"In my family and friends I have discovered treasure more valuable than gold."

Jimmy Buffet
American musician

QUESTIONS TO CONSIDER

- What occasion might have brought these people together for this photograph?

- Who are the people, and how are they related?

- Approximately when do you think the photo was taken? Why?

- If you could, what questions would you ask the people?

POSSIBLE OPENING LINES

- They didn't want to pose for that photo, and now they wish they hadn't...

- Fashions change over the years, but some things stay the same...

"If you were going to die soon and had only one phone call you could make, who would you call and what would you say? And why are you waiting?"

Stephen Levine
American author

IDEAS FOR WRITING

- Is the pay phone soon to disappear completely? In mid-2006 there were an estimated 219 million cell phone users in the United States alone. Do you think that cell phones will ever replace traditional phones completely? Why or why not?

- Many people now view cell phones as a necessity in life. Are they really necessary? Why or why not?

- Do cell phones help people become closer in their relationships—or farther apart? Explain.

- What are some of the positive and negative effects cell phones have had on people in the U.S.?

"Because of your smile, you make life more beautiful."

Thich Nhat Hanh
Vietnamese monk

IDEAS FOR WRITING

- Who could the boy be? Describe one typical day in his life, as you imagine it.

- Imagine the boy as a young man of 25. Describe him.

- A smile can be a powerful force. How?

- Imagine that the boy is Superman's distant cousin, Superchild. He has arrived on Earth from another planet and teamed up with Superman to fight evil all over the world. Write about one of their adventures.

"I just don't want to be the damsel in distress. I'll scream on the balcony, but you've got to let me do a little action here."

Kirsten Dunst
American actor

IDEAS FOR WRITING

What if...

- the woman on the balcony started singing to passers-by?

- the balcony railing came loose as the woman leaned against it?

- someone appeared on an adjacent balcony and threatened to jump?

- the woman accidentally (or on purpose!) let something fall from her hands?

- the woman had a habit of heckling passers-by?

- the woman were looking for someone?

"The #1 killer of teenagers doesn't have a trigger. It has a steering wheel."

advertisement in *Time* magazine

IDEAS FOR WRITING

- Although teenagers account for only 7% of the driving population in this country, they are involved in 14% of the accidents that are fatal. What do you think could help lower this figure?

- What special laws apply to teenage drivers in your state? Do you feel that they are necessary?

- Should it be illegal to use a cell phone while driving?

POSSIBLE KEY WORDS

TRAGEDY   WRECK   JUNK   SAFETY   DRIVER

> *"Graffiti is…a legitimate aesthetic and cultural movement, born of a revolutionary spirit and a will to resistance."*
>
> Antonio Zaya
> Spanish art critic

IDEAS FOR WRITING

- The photo shows graffiti in a modern setting. However, graffiti originated as what was then called "wall writing" long before Columbus discovered America. In fact, during Roman times, people scribbled such messages as "Successus was here," "I don't want to sell my husband," and "Burglar, watch out" on walls in the city of Pompeii. Do you believe that graffiti is a legitimate art form? Explain.

- What problems has graffiti caused in modern times?

- Describe examples of graffiti that exist where you live. Tell how people respond to it.

RESEARCH AND WRITE

- Find out more about the origin of graffiti and report on your findings.

"Just because something doesn't do what you planned it to do doesn't mean it's useless."

Thomas A. Edison
American inventor

POSSIBLE OPENING LINES

- The abandoned school bus looked like...

- How does a perfectly good school bus disappear for 30 years, without a trace?...

- I remember my old bus driver well...

- Most of the time, riding a school bus can be boring, but I can remember one day when...

- No one knew about that old bus, except for me...

POSSIBLE KEY WORDS

ABANDONED   RUSTING   FORLORN   STUCK   USELESS

"Be able to be alone."

Thomas Browne
British author

QUESTIONS TO CONSIDER

- Where is this woman going?

- Why is she alone?

- What mood does the photo suggest?

- What does the woman's posture reveal?

- What do the bars on the windows indicate?

- What might be just out of sight?

- What could she be carrying?

IDEAS FOR WRITING

- Who is the woman? Describe who you imagine her to be, and what she is like.

- Create a scene that involves the woman in the photo.

- What does it feel like to be alone?

"Our birthdays are feathers in the broad wing of time."

Jean Paul Richter
German author

IDEAS FOR WRITING

• Describe the girl in the photo. Who is she? Describe her birthday celebration.

• What was the most memorable birthday party you ever attended? In telling about it, include some or all of the following:

> Where was the party held?
> Who attended?
> What foods were served?
> What games did people play?
> What were some of your feelings while you were at the party?
> What happened at the party? Describe at least one incident.

• Describe your ideal birthday party.

> *"It's a man's world, and you men can have it."*
>
> Katherine Anne Porter
> American author

QUESTIONS TO CONSIDER

- Who do you think the men in the photo are?

- Why are they posing together?

- Why are there no women in the photo?

- Why might someone have this photo? What could be its importance?

IDEAS FOR WRITING

- Create a "background" for the photo. Imagine its history and describe it.

- Do you agree with the quotation, above, that "It's a man's world." Why or why not?

- Why do you think people have long talked, mostly in jest, about "running off to join the circus"? What is the attraction?

"What a lot we lost when we stopped writing letters. You can't reread a phone call."

Liz Carpenter
American author

IDEAS FOR WRITING

In countries in which the illiteracy rate is high, many people still communicate by writing letters rather than by sending text messages or e-mails. This photo shows a letter writer offering his services on a street corner in Peru. A small typewriter rests on a table in front of him.

- Imagine that you are either the man on the left or the woman on the right and that you are paying the letter writer to write a letter. Describe yourself. Who are you, and where do you live? Describe the person to whom you are writing, and tell why you are doing so.

- What are the contents of the dictated letter?

POSSIBLE OPENING LINES

- I have good news.

- I have bad news.

"...fighting not good. But when must fight, win."

Pat Morita as Mr. Miyagi
in *The Next Karate Kid*

IDEAS FOR WRITING

- What are the boys doing? Why?

- What if a third person jumped into the fighting area?

- What if an enraged parent decided to get into the action?

- Is fighting ever a good idea? Why or why not?

- Do you agree or disagree with the quotation above?

POSSIBLE OPENING LINES

- No one watching the fight could have known that...

- I thought the competition was going to be like any other competition, but...

- Everyone was surprised when...

"Just say no to plastic bags."
Bryan Walsh
American journalist

IDEAS FOR WRITING

- Imagine that you are the person in charge of the cart in the photo. Are you a custodian picking up trash? A homeless person hoping to find cans to turn in for money? Or...?

- Do you agree or disagree with the quotation above? Explain.

RESEARCH AND WRITE

Plastic (polyethylene) bags photodegrade over time and eventually contaminate soils and waterways.

- Find out more about the effects of plastic bags on our planet.

- Find out more about the causes of global warning and the effects on our planet. Describe one of the causes in detail and discuss possible solutions.

*"I don't know anything about music.
In my line you don't have to."*

Elvis Presley
American singer-musician

IDEAS FOR WRITING

• Describe as many similarities as you can between the two men.

• Describe, in detail, the differences between the two men.

• Each of the men plays his instrument of choice. What is your favorite musical instrument? Do you like to play it? Listen to it? Describe it in detail and give reasons why you like it.

• Write a scene between the two men, showing a distinct contrast in their characters.

• Describe your favorite singer, musician, or group.

"We are by nature all as one, all alike...let us wear theirs and they our clothes, and what is the difference?"

Robert Burton
British scholar

RESEARCH AND WRITE

Muslim women are not the only people who wear a *hijab*, or head covering. At one point in history some Jewish women wore head coverings that sometimes covered their faces. Roman Catholic nuns have been covering their heads for hundreds of years. And some Amish and Mennonite women still wear head coverings to this day.

Through the ages, many women have worn not only head coverings, but also clothing that covers their entire bodies.

- Find out more about the purpose of head coverings worn by women of different religions. Do head coverings have different meanings for different groups?

- Find out about other religious clothing requirements for women throughout the ages.

- What special religious clothing requirements have some men had throughout the ages?

"We've always been ready for female superheroes."

Famke Janssen
Dutch actress

IDEAS FOR WRITING

- Not as well known as Wonder Woman, Supergirl, or Catwoman, Avenger Woman is a descendant of the Aztec god Quitzelpickelpetal. By day she is an English teacher at a high school, where she is known as Ms. Consuela Hernandez. By night, she fights crime all over the world. Her last amazing adventure took place at the mall in your hometown, where she stopped Doctor No-No from committing an evil deed.

   What evil deed did she stop? And how did she do it?

- Compare and contrast Avenger Woman's appearance when she is Consuela Hernandez with her appearance in her role as a super heroine.

- Create another villain for Avenger Woman to battle.

POSSIBLE KEY WORDS

BRAVERY   ADVENTURE   DISGUISE   EVIL   BATTLE

Note: The photograph actually shows a section of a mural on a public building
in San Miguel de Allende, Mexico.

"There must always be a struggle between a father and son, while one aims at power and the other at independence."

Samuel Johnson
British author

IDEAS FOR WRITING

- From looking at the smiling faces in the photo, what kind of relationship do you imagine the father and son have? Describe it.

- How do relationships between parents and children change as the children mature? Why?

- Everyone has seen a conflict between a parent and a child, even in the most loving families. Describe a conflict you have witnessed or experienced firsthand.

POSSIBLE OPENING LINES

- Like father, like son? It's not true...

- Like father, like son? It's true...

- Hal admired his father, but...

"Those who cannot remember the past are condemned to repeat it."

George Santayana
American philosopher

IDEAS FOR WRITING

- From the details in the photo, what do you know is probably true about the man pictured? Describe him.

- Describe what you think he would be like if he were living today.

- You have undoubtedly read stories and seen television shows and movies about life before we had television sets, cell phones, and jet planes. Do you think life was better or worse than it is now? Explain.

- Do you agree or disagree with Santayana's quotation, above? Why or why not?

POSSIBLE OPENING LINES

- Henry posed for a historic photo...

- My great-grandfather was an interesting man...

"How come the dove gets to be the peace symbol?..."

Jack Handy
American writer

IDEAS FOR WRITING

- What is your interpretation of this photograph? Turn it upside down and sideways for different views. What is it? What could it mean? How and where was it taken?

- Discuss this image with at least three other people. Then summarize their interpretations of the image.

- Imagine that the image is a symbol of some kind. What could it symbolize?

- Imagine that this is a newly discovered animal. Describe it.

"Listen! you hear the grating roar
Of pebbles which the waves draw back, and fling,
At their return, up the high strand.
Begin, and cease, and then again begin..."

from "Dover Beach"
Matthew Arnold
British poet

IDEAS FOR WRITING

• People often become lost in their thoughts at the ocean. What could be the reasons for that?

• Imagine what the boy might be thinking. Describe his thoughts.

• Whether you realize it or not, you are developing a philosophy of life that is uniquely yours. Describe one of your beliefs.

• Write a poem about the ocean. If you like, fashion it after the style of the poem in the quotation, above.

POSSIBLE KEY WORDS

MEDITATE   REFLECT   CONTEMPLATE   CONSIDER

"All walking is discovery."

Hal Borland
American author

IDEAS FOR WRITING

- What are the first thoughts that come to mind when you see this photograph? Who could the man be? Where could he be going?

- Describe the man and his surroundings.

- According to the quotation above, all walking is discovery. Do you agree or disagree?

POSSIBLE OPENING LINES

- There was purpose in the man's walk...

- A man in a long, black coat walked toward the...

*"The parade is marching down the street.
I think the band sounds really neat."*

Debbie Clement
American educator/singer-songwriter

IDEAS FOR WRITING

- Many people love parades. What is it about a parade that attracts people?

- You've probably heard the advice not to let it "rain on your parade." What does that advice mean?

- Imagine that all the spectators at a parade suddenly disappeared. Describe the effect on the parade participants.

- Write a story in which a parade is the basis for the plot. What will be the conflict in your story? How will you resolve it?

"How much of human life is lost in waiting."

Ralph Waldo Emerson
American poet

IDEAS FOR WRITING

- Look at the shadows in the photo. How do they contribute to the mood of the scene?

- What does it feel like to wait for someone who is always late?

- In your opinion, how important is it for people to be on time?

- In some cultures, time is not as important as it is in the U.S. How would your life be different if it were not important at all to be anywhere at a designated time?

POSSIBLE KEY WORDS

WAIT   LANGUISH   EXPECT   ANTICIPATE

"I am a woman above all else."

Jacqueline Kennedy Onassis
former First Lady

IDEAS FOR WRITING

- The woman on the left is from Portugal. The woman on the right is from Spain. Compare and contrast the women. Look at clothing, expression, posture, setting, emotion, and anything else that seems relevant.

- Imagine that the two women meet and are able to talk to one another about something more than just the time of day. Write the conversation you can imagine them having.

"Photography takes an instant out of time, altering life by holding it still."

Dorothea Lange
American documentary photojournalist

IDEAS FOR WRITING

• What does the little girl see? What could she be trying to capture?

• Does a photograph always show the truth?

• How can a photograph get someone into trouble?

POSSIBLE OPENING LINES

• Later, the Dunns were very, very sorry they had given Alissa a camera for Christmas...

• No one could have imagined that a photograph would save the day...

"Make voyages! Attempt them...there's nothing else."

Tennessee Williams
American playwright

IDEAS FOR WRITING

- What story might lie behind this photo? Tell it.

- If you could travel anywhere in the world, where would you go, and what would you do after you got there? Give specific reasons for your choices.

POSSIBLE KEY WORDS

ADVENTURE   IRONY   VOYAGE   TRAVEL

"Be curious, not judgmental."

Walt Whitman
American poet

IDEAS FOR WRITING

- Describe the woman in a *kind* manner. Don't judge her or criticize her. Describe her in a way that the reader will feel sympathetic toward her. Perhaps your description will include some of her background or history.

- Imagine that the woman finds something important in the trash—perhaps a credit card, a weapon wrapped in a newspaper, or a purse or backpack containing a wallet and a set of keys. What does she find? What does she do with what she finds?

- What would you do if you found $1,000 in a paper bag that did not contain any form of identification?

*"She caught the train she said she would,
And changed at junctions as she should."*

Rose Henniker-Heaton
British writer

IDEAS FOR WRITING

- If you look closely, you will see that the photo shows a train station. What time of day do you think it is? Where is the station? Where might most of the people be going? Is there anyone in the photo who doesn't seem to belong? Describe the scene.

RESEARCH AND WRITE

Because it reaches heights of 13,000 feet above sea level, the Peruvian Central Railway carries an onboard doctor to administer oxygen to passengers who need it. And the Shinkansen high-speed trains in Japan are able to reach speeds of 130 mph. Find out more about at least two of the following trains and tell what makes each unique:

- Peruvian Central Railway (Peru)
- Shinkansen high-speed trains (Japan)
- Orient-Express (Europe)
- Indian Pacific (Australia)
- TGV (France)
- 20th Century Limited (United States)

"The thoughtful soul to solitude retires."

Omar Khayyám
Persian scholar

IDEAS FOR WRITING

Imagine what the young man is thinking about, and describe his thoughts. Is he thinking about...

- a problem at school?
- his girlfriend?
- his religion?
- a problem in his family?
- a choice he has to make?

- how his friends see him?
- something that makes him feel guilty?
- something that makes him happy?
- or...?

POSSIBLE OPENING LINES

- Martin was a worrier...

- Derek fooled everyone when he stared off into space...

"Whether it's the best of times or the worst of times, it's the only time we've got."

Art Buchwald
American humorist

IDEAS FOR WRITING

- Is it true that we see what we *want* to see? How does the photo support that statement?

- What would happen if a watch or clock were able to describe things that it has seen?

- Imagine what it would be like to live in a place that pays no attention to time. How would your life be different?

POSSIBLE OPENING LINES

- Jeanette was surprised when the watch she was wearing actually began to speak to her...

- Yes, I'm the one who invented a time machine...

"Alone, all alone
Nobody, but nobody,
Can make it out here alone."

Maya Angelou
American poet

IDEAS FOR WRITING

- Describe the man. What does his facial expression and body language tell you? What is he thinking? What is he feeling?

- Give the man a history. Who could he be? What is his background? Where is he going?

- Comment on Maya Angelou's quotation. What do you think she means? Do you agree or disagree?

POSSIBLE KEY WORDS

ALONE   FEARFUL   DETERMINED   GRIM   PURPOSEFUL

"Are you really sure that a floor can't also be a ceiling?"

M.C. Escher
Dutch graphic artist

IDEAS FOR WRITING

- What is the man in the photo doing? First describe what is happening, putting a negative spin on the man's actions. Then describe what is happening in such a way that the actions seem positive.

- Discuss the M.C. Escher quotation, above. What do you think Escher means?

POSSIBLE OPENING LINES

- The man saw that the window was open...

- Luckily, Joseph came by when he did...

- On Tuesday, Mr. Gomez was grateful for the help of a stranger...

- After Tuesday, Mr. Gomez knew he would never again leave the windows unlocked...

"Old age is no place for sissies."

Bette Davis
American actress

IDEAS FOR WRITING

- Why is this woman standing on the street holding a bouquet of flowers?

- Create a history for the woman. Who is she? What is her background? What was life like for her as a younger woman?

- Has a senior adult influenced your life in some way, either positively or negatively? Explain.

- What difficulties might the woman be facing as an older adult? Imagine some problems that she faces.

"Let's face it, the cheapest energy is the energy you don't use in the first place."

Sheryl Crow
American singer-songwriter

IDEAS FOR WRITING

• Although the United States contains just 5% of the world's population, Americans consume 26% of the world's energy. As if that figure were not bad enough, scientists predict that it will increase 17% by the year 2015. Discuss several ways in which you, your family, and your friends can help to conserve energy and not be "oinkers."

• What is one of the most wasteful uses of energy that you have seen?

RESEARCH AND WRITE

• Some methods of producing energy are less harmful to the environment than those that are currently in use. Choose at least two of the following methods. What are the advantages of each? The disadvantages?

solar power
thermal power
wind power
nuclear power

"People only see what they are prepared to see."

Ralph Waldo Emerson
American poet

QUESTIONS TO CONSIDER

• Why is the man carrying an umbrella?

• Why is he touching the frame of the door?

• What is inside the darkened doorway?

• What is the man thinking as he stands in the doorway?

• What will he do after he passes through the doorway?

POSSIBLE OPENING LINES

• Jerry hesitated and took a deep breath before stepping inside the store...

• The man was nervous. Very nervous...

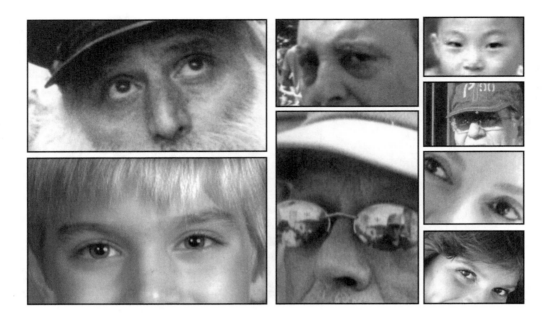

*"Away, and mock the time with fairest show;
False face must hide what the false heart doth know."*
William Shakespeare
Dramatist and poet

IDEAS FOR WRITING

- Choose one set of eyes above, and create a character sketch of the person. What do you think the person is like, based on the eyes?

- The Shakespeare quotation above comes from the play *Macbeth*. Macbeth indicates that, although he plans to kill King Duncan, he must appear to be friendly so that he will be able to mask his intentions. What intentions could some of the people in the photos be masking? What secret thoughts could they be harboring?

POSSIBLE OPENING LINES

- If anyone finds out...

- You'll never know that...

- No one must ever know that...

"I love to see a young girl go out and grab the world by the lapels."

Maya Angelou
American poet

IDEAS FOR WRITING

- If we are observant, photos can tell us a lot about a person. What can you guess about the little girl, based only on the photos?

- Create a fictional scene involving the girl. Give her a name and a problem to solve. How will she solve the problem?

- What does it mean for a young girl to "grab the world by the lapels"?

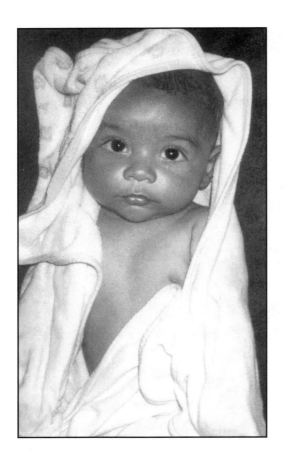

"A new baby is like the beginning of all things—wonder, hope, a dream of possibilities."

Eda J. Le Shan
American psychologist

QUESTIONS TO CONSIDER

- What could the baby be seeing and thinking as it looks at the world through innocent eyes?

- How is the baby's view likely to change as it grows older and matures?

- Is the baby a boy or a girl? How will its gender affect what it sees and thinks?

IDEA FOR WRITING

Write an essay from the point of view of the baby as it reflects on one or more of the questions above.

"Two men look out through the same bars: One sees the mud and one the stars."

Frederick Langbridge
British clergyman-author

POSSIBLE OPENING LINES

- As I looked up, I felt that anything could happen if I...

- Some people thought that the buildings looked dangerous. I thought...

- Anne balanced on the beams, like a tightrope walker...

- "You're crazy if you think I'm going into that building," said Trent.

> *"Science may have found a cure for most evils; but it has found no remedy for the worst of them all—the apathy of human beings."*
>
> Helen Keller
> American author, activist and lecturer

IDEAS FOR WRITING

- The man in the photo seems oblivious to the large sign advertising a vacation in Mexico. Imagine that the people in the photo get his attention by coming to life. What would they say to him?

- Discuss Helen Keller's quotation. Do you agree that apathy is an "evil"? Are there different kinds of apathy?

POSSIBLE OPENING LINES

- "Wake up! Look! We're offering you a trip to Mexico," the women shouted...

- Gordon didn't really care about anything except what was going on inside his head...

*"A good snapshot stops a
moment from running away."*
Eudora Welty
American author

IDEAS FOR WRITING

- Imagine what the woman in the picture might be photographing. Describe what she sees.

- Discuss Eudora Welty's quotation, above. What does she mean? How important are photographs? What do they mean to you?

POSSIBLE OPENING LINES

- She couldn't believe her eyes. Maybe what they said about the Loch Ness monster was true...

- Just as she got close enough to snap the picture...

"All I ask is that you respect me as a human being."

Jackie Robinson
American baseball player

IDEAS FOR WRITING

- Do you agree that if you give respect, you get it? Explain.

- Of all the people you know, who is the person you respect most of all? Why? What has the person done to earn your respect?

- What actions do *you* take to earn the respect of others?

RESEARCH AND WRITE

- Jackie Robinson, whose quotation appears above, was an African-American baseball player who ended approximately eighty years of baseball segregation when he signed on with the Brooklyn Dodgers in 1947. Find out more about the difficulties he faced in breaking this color barrier.

"Perhaps the truth depends on a walk around the lake."

Wallace Stevens
American poet

IDEAS FOR WRITING

- Who are the boys, and what are they doing?

- When you were younger, did you have an older relative, neighbor, or friend that you looked up to? Who was it, and what did you like so much about the person?

POSSIBLE OPENING LINES

- William looked down at his little brother and said, "Now you can tell me. What's wrong?"...

- The boys stood at the lake for hours, watching and waiting...

POSSIBLE KEY WORDS

BROTHERS   TRUTH   SUMMER   SHARING

"The sun shines and warms and lights us and we have no curiosity to know why this is so; but we ask the reason of all evil, of pain, and hunger, and mosquitoes and silly people."

Ralph Waldo Emerson
American poet, lecturer and essayist

IDEAS FOR WRITING

- If you were an observer at this scene, what would you be thinking?

- Using words and sentences rather than watercolor or oil, create a description of the scene.

POSSIBLE OPENING LINES

- The scene was breathtaking, with...

- The light reflected on the water made me think of...

- Rochelle simply stared at the scene...

POSSIBLE KEY WORDS

REFLECTIONS   LIGHT   IMAGINATION   SPARKLES

"Every doorway, every intersection has a story."

Katherine Dunn
American author

IDEAS FOR WRITING

- According to the quotation above, every doorway has a story. Tell the story of the doorway in the photo.

- What doorways have led to changes in your life?

- Is there a doorway you love to go through? Why?

- Is there a doorway you dread going through? Why?

- Where does the doorway to your future lead?

POSSIBLE KEY WORDS

APPREHENSIVE   EAGER   EXPECTANT   CURIOUS   HESITANT

"Children are the world's most valuable resource and its best hope for the future."

John F. Kennedy
35th President of the United States

IDEAS FOR WRITING

- The children seem to be looking directly at the camera. Who do you think they are? Where are they? What might they be thinking?

- If children are the best hope for the future, what can we do to help them prepare for that future?

POSSIBLE OPENING LINES

- The children gathered around the photographer, curious...

- Children are the same, everywhere...

> *"All ages before ours believed in gods in some form or another."*
>
> Carl Jung
> Swiss psychiatrist

RESEARCH AND WRITE

The photo shows a forty-two-foot high replica in Nashville, Tennessee, of the Greek goddess Athena. History tells us that many ancient religions were based on polytheism, or the belief in the existence of many gods and goddesses. But did you know that a significant number of the modern world's religions remain polytheistic? Some examples are Hinduism, Mahayana Buddhism, Confucianism, Taoism, Shintoism, and several tribal religions in Africa and the Americas.

Choose a polytheistic religion you are not very familiar with and find out more about the gods and goddesses of that religion.

HOW SOME TEACHERS USE PHOTOGRAPHS TO INSPIRE WRITING

"Words and pictures can work together to communicate more powerfully than either alone."

William Albert Allard
American photographer

Many teachers across the country have already discovered the power of using photographs to inspire writing. Below, a number of them share ideas that have been successful for them. Perhaps some of these ideas will inspire *you*.

Comparing two photos. In one photo-related exercise that he uses, English teacher Martin Brandt shows his students at Independence High School, San Jose, California, side-by-side photos of two women and asks them to respond in writing to the following five questions: (1) What does each photograph *show*? (2) How is each woman *dressed*? (3) What do you notice about the *environment* of each woman? (4) What do you notice about the *condition* of each woman? (5) What do the two women have in *common*?

Norma Jean, aka Marilyn Monroe. From the Boston Writing Project, Peter Golden reports that in one of several photo-related exercises he uses with students at South Boston High School, he projects a photo of Marilyn Monroe (a Norma Jean photo) and asks the students to write down their responses and share them. After the students arrive at a general description of the subject, as in shy or sophisticated, Golden presses them for details. Then he directs them to write descriptions of Norma that convey their conclusion (shy or sophisticated) without using that word. "In other words," he writes, "the reader should come to the same conclusion just by reading the description."

Bridges. At the University of Alabama, Diane Sekeres used photographs of bridges as prompts in a workshop she conducted at a Longleaf Writing Project Summer Institute for teachers. "I found about 20 pictures of different kinds of bridges: rope, draw, suspension, destroyed, over gorges, over highways, over water, for example," she writes. "Then I asked the teachers to study the photos and select one that was a metaphor for their teaching." At the conclusion to the exercise, the teacher-students wrote about their choices and their reasons for making them.

Multi-genre presentations and portfolios. At the University of Mississippi Writing Project, Allison Movitz's students use their own photographs to spark writings of various kinds. The students also incorporate their photos into autobiographical, multi-genre presentations and portfolios. "Most recently," writes Movitz, "we've used Microsoft's PhotoStory 3, a digital camera, and a microphone to re-create a 'who done it' from a mock trial in speech/debate classes."

Poetry. After having students respond to several photos in terms of the five senses, Lehigh Valley Writing Project co-director Kristy Weidner-Gonzalez has the students write short poems in which each line reveals one of the senses. Then the students take a walking tour of the school and surrounding neighborhood during which they photograph their favorite places. Using the images they produced, the students revisit the idea of senses as they write about what they had experienced when they created the photos. "The second time around has much more meaning for the students," writes Weidner-Gonzalez, "because the places they photographed were much more personal and held certain memories for them."

Memory vs. reality. Iowa Writing Project director James Davis asks his students to recall a photograph of some significance to them. Then he directs them to describe the photograph as they remember it. "Who is in the photograph?" he asks. "What are their expressions and stances? What are the important details of the setting?" Davis then asks the students to find the photograph they described and study it carefully before writing about any discrepancies between the photograph as it exists and their memory of it. "Why might these discrepancies exist?" he concludes. "Which version has more to do with truth?"

Painting with words. Mary Birky is an English teacher at the Papillion-La Vista High School, Papillion, Nebraska; a Nebraska Writing Project Advisory Board Member; and a contributor to a forthcoming book on place-conscious education. Birky uses student-generated photos to stimulate writing assignments based on the content of the photos, the mood of the photos, and the imagery in the photos. "I tell them to 'paint the photograph with words,'" she writes, before she asks them to create free-verse poetry based on the phrases they have selected.

Characterization. As a teacher consultant for the Illinois State Writing Project and English teacher at Central Catholic High School in Bloomington, Ann Cox uses photos to teach characterization. After giving her students a magazine photo of a person, she asks them to write a character sketch of the person. Then she provides a scenario and directs the students to describe how their characters would react and why. Finally, students share their writing with the class and discuss their characters' motivation.

Purpose and audience. "One of the projects my students and parents are most proud of is a project I do with my high school freshmen," writes Jennifer Sluss, tech liaison for the Mountain Writing Project at Hazard Community and Technical College, Hazard, Kentucky. To help teach purpose and audience in writing, Sluss's students create visual personal narratives/memoirs that she fondly refers to as the Me Mini Movie. In this exercise, students compile photos that tell a story or present an aspect of their lives that they value. "We then add a song to the photos in Movie Maker or PowerPoint. When we do this, the students must focus on matching the music to their message. We also talk about tone, audience, and the purpose of the Me Mini Movies." Sluss also uses representations of abstract art to help her junior English students relate to the themes and plots of novels.

"I Am From" poems. At the Prairie Lands Writing Project in St. Joseph, Missouri, teacher consultant Mary Lee Meyer asks her high school students to write "I Am From" poems based on photos that are significant to them in terms of their lives. To support this activity, she asks such questions as *Where are you from? Who are/were your grandparents or great grandparents? What occupations did some of your ancestors have?* Meyer has also used this exercise at a writing institute for teachers. You can see samples at:

www.missouriwestern.edu/plwp/wtca/examples.htm
(under "Writing Marathon Example 1 Addie")
and
www.missouriwestern.edu/plwp/wtca/examples.htm
(under I Am From...poem "Example 1 Michele.")

Stories about children. Frank Holes, Jr. is the editor of *Star Teaching* and an English teacher at Inland Lakes Middle School, Indian River, Michigan. Holes shows his students photographs of children performing daily activities and asks them such questions as *Who is the child? What is his/her name? What is the subject's family like? How old is the subject? What is he or she feeling?* "I also ask the students to give a full description of the setting that includes sense impressions," writes Holes. Then he asks questions related to a possible plot before he directs the students to write a story that places the child in the setting.

Analyzing photo essays. "Photo essays tell stories with pictures in ways that words cannot," writes Kathy Miller, a teacher consultant at the Prairie Lands Writing Project. In one of her photo-related exercises, Miller directs her students at West Platte High School, Weston, Missouri to select three photo essays from the Internet, study them, and analyze them in terms of written responses to such questions as (1) Do the photos in the essays stand alone? (2) How much narration supports the photos? (3) How does the narration complement or support the photos? (4) What are your responses to the essays? In another exercise, Miller uses Brian Lanker's *I Dream a World* as a source of photos of African-American women. "I direct students to select a photo, study it, and relate how the woman in the photo they chose is like them or different," she concludes.

Family photos. At the Ottawa Elementary School, Petoskey, Michigan, Alisa Santti uses family photos to connect with her students' lives. "We ask the students to bring in photos showing family-oriented activities," she writes. "Then we encourage them to write descriptive paragraphs that reveal more than just what is plainly seen in the photos. To this end, we urge them to generate ideas in terms of who, what, where, when, and how." In another activity, Santti uses postcards or photos of various places as triggers for descriptive paragraphs. "After they write their descriptions," she concludes, "the students read them to their classmates who must then draw pictures based on what they've heard."

Memoirs. In her classes at California State University at Monterey Bay and at Cabrillo College, Barbara Raney directs her students to read Richard Rodriguez' essay about a photo display in San Francisco. "In this essay," she writes, "Rodriguez asserts that anyone with a camera can create meaningful images." Then Raney shows the students photos of her grandparents, aunts, uncles, and other relatives and asks them to write memoirs based on photos of their own relatives. "The students do a good job of speculating about how/why their subjects changed since the photographs were taken," she concludes.

Narration. In Brooklyn Park, Minnesota, adjunct instructor of English Amber Luck promotes narrative writing by showing her students at Hennepin Technical College photographs depicting people in situations in which it isn't immediately clear what's happening. "The assignment," she writes, "is for each student to choose one person in one of the photos and write the story behind the picture from that person's point of view." Students then take turns reading their stories aloud to their classmates. "The results are often hilarious," concludes Luck, "and the assignment works as a community-building exercise, as well as an introduction to narration."

Elements of fiction. At Kalamazoo Valley Community College in Kalamazoo, Michigan, Linda Dick uses many interesting and exciting techniques to help her students create stories, poems, and expository pieces. In her creative writing classes, for example, she asks them to collect an image file: a folder full of magazine images and/or Internet images of anything. "In the classroom," she writes, "I ask the students to choose one of the images. Then I direct some of them to write a biography, others to write up a scene, and still others to create a plot line." Finally, the students put everything together spontaneously. "In that way," concludes Dick, "they learn a great deal about the elements of fiction."

Easing intimidation. "To spur on students who are afraid to write, or intimidated by the writing process," writes Derri Scarlett, "I have them take pictures (or bring in pictures) that they like." An English instructor at Bismarck State College, Bismarck, North Dakota, Scarlett then encourages those students to talk about why they like the photos, or what the photos mean to them. Then she directs the students to "brainstorm" on paper. That's when they jot down the words they first spoke of when they discussed the photographs. From that exercise come sentences, then an essay. "Because the students have invested themselves in the subject matter," concludes Scarlett, "this is a great way of easing into the writing process."

"Found" photographs. At Southwestern Oklahoma State University, Weatherford, Oklahoma, Valerie Reimers cites noted photography critic and historian A.D. Coleman's love of "found" photographs, which he sometimes picks up inexpensively in antique stores. "In conjunction with the idea of 'found' photographs," she writes, "Coleman suggests that writing workshop participants bring favorite photos to class." Then the students exchange photos and write about their borrowed photos as if they had just found a very interesting photo and are describing it. "Looking at someone else's photo brings attention to details that might be ignored as too familiar in one's own favorite photo," Reimers concludes. Students then share what they have written about each other's photos before they write about their own images.

The digital age. "Now that we are in the digital age," writes Coastal Georgia Writing Project director Patricia West, "I have students in my college freshman composition course take photographs to support an observational writing essay. Then we conduct campus writing marathons to get the students familiar with the process." West also uses family photos to help generate writings about heritage. In another exercise, West sparks critical thinking by showing students Henry O. Tanner's painting *The Banjo Lesson* and asking the question, "Who is teaching whom?"

Memory snapshots. Carol Booth Olson is the director of the UCI Writing Project (University of California, Irvine), a member of the National Writing Project Advisory Board, and the author of *The Reading/Writing Connection*. Olson has created a "memory snapshot" exercise for use with her students. First she asks them to select photographs that they associate with significant memories. Then she directs them to create written snapshots that capture a "You are there" feeling in the reader by using rich sensory details. "I point out that the goal is not to tell about the event but to show what is happening by dramatizing the event," she writes.

Towns. English teacher Joann Garbarini shows her students at Irvine High School in Irvine, California, photographs of different towns and asks them to pick one they would like to write about. She then instructs them to imagine what the town they chose is like. "They must include descriptions of ethnicities, social class, jobs, relationships between neighbors, the education system, the town's history, and anything else they can surmise from the photograph," she writes. To conclude the exercise, Garbarini directs the students to write about their own town and compare and contrast it to their imaginary town.

Animal inspiration. Justin Van Kleeck's very successful photo-related writing activity with students he tutors involves showing them the photo of a baby macaque and a pigeon who had "adopted" each other as friends: http://primatology.net/2007/09/13/baby-macaque-and-white-pigeon-make-friends. "I ask my students to freewrite after showing them the photo and giving them information about the background story of how the animals came together," he writes. A former adjunct assistant professor of English at Piedmont Virginia Community College, he then allows the students to write about anything in the picture that interests them, from how different species can get along so easily while humans often cannot, to the human behaviors that stress animals, such as poaching.

He also shows his students a video of a seagull that steals a bag of Doritos from a store in Scotland every day. In the first part of the assignment, he directs the students to write a process paper in which they instruct their fellow seagulls on how to steal, open, and eat the Doritos. In the second part of the assignment, he tells the students to write from the point of view of a shopkeeper who is telling other shopkeepers how to prevent the seagull from stealing Doritos in a creative, nonviolent way. "The key to the exercise," concludes Van Kleeck, "is for students to utilize the process approach while also employing their imaginations. They should be encouraged to create easy to follow, step-by-step instructions without skimping on style."